★ ★

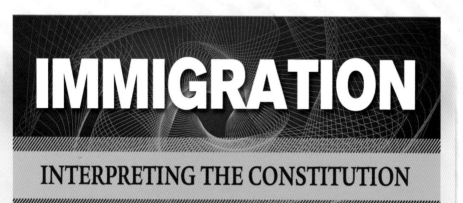

IMMIGRATION

INTERPRETING THE CONSTITUTION

ANN BYERS

ROSEN
PUBLISHING ®

New York

Published in 2015 by The Rosen Publishing Group, Inc.
29 East 21st Street, New York, NY 10010

Copyright © 2015 by The Rosen Publishing Group, Inc.

First Edition

Library of Congress Cataloging-in-Publication Data

Byers, Ann, author.
Immigration : interpreting the Constitution/Ann Byers.
    pages cm. — (Understanding the United States Constitution)
Includes bibliographical references and index.
ISBN 978-1-4777-7512-7 (library bound)
1. Emigration and immigration law—United States—Juvenile literature. 2. Emigration and immigration—Political aspects—United States—Juvenile literature. 3. Citizenship—United States—Juvenile literature. 4. Immigrants—United States—Juvenile literature. 5. Illegal aliens—United States—Juvenile literature. I. Title.
KF4819.85.B94 2015
342.7308'2—dc23

                                            2013038832

Manufactured in China

CONTENTS

INTRODUCTION

Elvira Arellano stands with her American-born son inside a Chicago church where she sought protection as an illegal immigrant. In her arm she holds a speech she will deliver at a press conference about immigrant rights.

G etting into the United States was easy. A turn-stile at the border crossing was unguarded just long enough for Elvira Arellano to walk unchallenged from Mexico to the United States. Getting to America had been a dream for twenty-two-year-old Arellano, according to articles in *Time* and *USA TODAY*. Life in Mexico was hard for the family. Arellano's ill father could no longer work in the fields. If she could get to the United States, she reasoned, she could get a job, earn a decent living, and help her family.

But shortly after her first attempt, Arellano was arrested and sent back. On her second try, she made it. For five years Arellano experienced the typical life of many illegal immigrants. She lived in predominantly immigrant neighborhoods, spoke almost no English, and held low-paying jobs. Still, as a janitor cleaning the planes at Chicago's O'Hare Airport, she was on her way to realizing her dream.

After the terrorist attacks of September 11, 2001, everything changed for Arellano. In an attempt to improve security, the federal government swept through some airports, arresting people who did not have papers proving their right to be in the country. Arellano was one of fifty-three immigrants caught at O'Hare in 2002. Not only was she in the country illegally, but she had also used a false Social Security card. Because of that crime, she was to be deported.

But Arellano had a son who was born in the United States. According to the Fourteenth Amendment, four-year-old Saul was an American citizen. Arellano could take him with her to Mexico, but she wanted him to have the opportunities available in America, and she wanted to stay with him. She was able to have her removal postponed several times but was finally ordered to appear for deportation in 2006.

Instead, she sought sanctuary, or safety, in a church. Her sympathetic pastor gave her shelter. For a year Arellano lived in the church, and immigration officials did not go in after her. She and other activists made speeches and held vigils and demonstrations to garner support for changing immigration law. Eventually, Arellano drove to Los Angeles for a rally, and she was arrested and deported. Saul remained in Chicago.

Arellano's story illustrates some of the issues in today's attempt to revamp immigration laws and procedures. The debate is largely a question of what to do about illegal immigration. An estimated 11.7 million immigrants live in the United States illegally, according to the Pew Research Center Hispanic Trends Project. Many of them have children who were born in the United States and are therefore U.S. citizens.

Some issues are economic. On the one hand, illegal immigrants contribute to the nation's economy, and on the other hand, they use public services, which are costly. Security is a concern, as people intent on harm may enter illegally. Some see moral issues. Does America have an obligation to share its resources with people who have little or are oppressed? And there are political considerations. Who will get the immigrants' votes if and when they become citizens? How will others vote?

These were not always the primary concerns in the immigration debate. Since before America became a nation, disagreements about immigration have often surfaced, but the sources of those differences have changed over time. The issues have largely been shaped by the attitudes and conditions of the times.

CHAPTER ONE

CITIZENSHIP

Immigration is a two-part concern. It involves residency, or who can live in the United States, and citizenship, or who has what privileges and protections. During the colonial period, England made decisions about these matters. After independence, the leaders of the new nation struggled with the question of who should determine whether someone was an American citizen and what criteria they should use.

EARLY POLICIES

Under the Articles of Confederation, the first document laying out how the United States would function, the question of citizenship rested with each state. The document was an agreement among the states, so each state made its own rules. All the states accepted that "natural-born" residents were citizens, but the states had different processes for how someone born on foreign soil could become a citizen. Pennsylvania made people wait a year before granting them citizenship, whereas the wait in South Carolina was two years and in Georgia seven years. In Maryland, only those who swore they believed in the Christian religion could be naturalized, or given the same "privileges and immunities" as natural-born citizens. Some states demanded documentation of the immigrant's good character.

The differences in naturalization requirements among the states created problems when people traveled to other states. Each state had to accept citizens of other states as citizens of its own. James Madison pointed out some of the difficulties in *The Federalist 42*. For one, the Articles used the terms "free inhabitants" and "free citizens" interchangeably. Did that mean that an inhabitant of New York who had not lived there long enough to become a citizen of New York could be declared a citizen of Virginia if he moved there? If he moved back to New York, was he then a citizen of New York because he had been declared a citizen of Virginia? The Constitution cleared up the problem.

ONE NATION, ONE RULE

The delegates to the Constitutional Convention of 1787 agreed to transfer the responsibility for decisions about citizenship from the states to the federal government. They recognized the need for a uniform rule, one that would be the same throughout all the states. Therefore in Article I, Section 8, the part of the Constitution that enumerates, or lists, the specific powers of the new Congress, they wrote, "The Congress shall have power . . . to establish a uniform rule of naturalization."

In 1790, the year after the Constitution went into effect, Congress created its first uniform rule of naturalization. The Naturalization Act established a residency requirement: an alien had to reside in the country for two years before applying to become a citizen. This provision would give ample time for the prospective citizen to learn the ways of the new country.

The act specified two other requirements for naturalization: the individual had to be a "free white person" of "good character." This wording prohibited Native Americans, blacks (whether slaves or free men),

This 1940 painting depicts the signing of the Constitution at the Constitutional Convention, held from May 25 to September 17, 1787. George Washington, president of the convention, is standing at the desk.

and Asians from becoming citizens. It also excluded indentured servants, white persons who were not free because they had agreed to work for someone who supported them financially. The Naturalization Act, like all immigration laws, reflected the thinking of the times. America's leaders in 1790 believed that only people of European descent were capable of making good decisions and could therefore be trusted with the rights and duties of citizens.

However, public opinion turned against immigrants, even immigrants of European descent, when many people fleeing the French Revolution came to America in the 1790s. Some Americans feared the newcomers' radical ideas. In response, Congress passed a new Naturalization Act in 1795, extending the waiting period for citizenship to five years.

Then the discussion turned political. Two political parties dominated in early U.S. history: the Federalists and the Democratic-Republicans, also called Jeffersonians after their leader. The Federalists noticed that the newly naturalized immigrants tended to vote with the Jeffersonians. So the Federalists made it harder to become naturalized. They passed a third Naturalization Act in 1798, hiking the residency requirement to fourteen years. When the Jeffersonians returned to power, they replaced the Federalist law with the Naturalization Act of 1802. The new

BECOMING A CITIZEN

Today, immigrants are eligible for naturalization if they have "good moral character," do not have a criminal record, and have been legal permanent residents for at least five years (three years if married to a citizen). They must pass a civics exam and a test of English proficiency.

Applicants can study the hundred-question exam ahead of time. At the exam, an interviewer asks ten of the one hundred questions, and the applicant must answer six correctly. The English test involves speaking, reading, and writing. The applicant must be able to answer the interviewer's questions, read one of three sentences correctly aloud, and write the same sentence as the interviewer dictates it.

Once applicants successfully complete the examination, they take an oath of allegiance to the United States. That completes the naturalization process.

A woman holds a certificate showing that she has become a U.S. citizen. According to the Department of Homeland Security, more than 750,000 people became naturalized citizens in 2012 alone.

legislation returned the waiting period to five years, where it remains today.

Thus, by 1790, Congress had established two ways for a person to be declared a citizen: by being born in the United States or by naturalization according to legislative rules. An exception was made in 1848 with the Treaty of Guadalupe Hidalgo, which ended the Mexican-American War. Nearly eighty thousand people were granted U.S. citizenship when the lands in which they resided became part of the United States.

NATURAL-BORN CITIZENS

Citizenship matters because citizens are entitled to certain privileges and protections not guaranteed to others. The Naturalization Acts set rules for making aliens citizens, but neither the legislation nor the Constitution were clear about who else could be considered citizens. Although it might seem obvious that anyone born in a country is a citizen of that country, the Founding Fathers treated some people born in the United States as noncitizens. They thought of Native Americans as foreigners, and they gave slaves no legal protections. In most states, people who did not own land—and therefore did not pay taxes— could not vote.

The 1857 *Dred Scott* decision brought the first clarification of who was not a citizen. The Supreme Court ruled that an African American, whether slave or free, was "not a 'citizen' within the meaning of the Constitution of the United States." The judges reasoned,

Dred Scott, born into slavery, lost his appeal for his freedom in a 7–2 Supreme Court ruling. A few months later, he was returned to his original owners, who freed him.

"When the Constitution was adopted, they were not regarded in any of the States as members of the community which constituted the State, and were not numbered among its 'people or citizens.' Consequently, the special rights and immunities guaranteed to citizens do not apply to them."

That opinion remained in force for nine more years. After the Civil War, during the period of Reconstruction, many congressmen wanted to ensure that the newly freed African Americans were no longer treated as slaves. They passed the Civil Rights Act of 1866, which stated, "All persons born in the United States and not subject to any foreign power, excluding Indians not taxed, are hereby declared to be citizens of the United States."

But would someone challenge the law as unconstitutional based on the Supreme Court's ruling in the *Dred Scott* case? Would Southern states find ways to get around the law? To ensure that African Americans would be protected, a congressional committee drafted an amendment to the Constitution that contained the heart of the Civil Rights Act. Before the states that had rebelled in the Civil War could be readmitted to the Union, they had to ratify the amendment. In 1868, the Fourteenth Amendment became part of the Constitution.

A DEBATABLE DEFINITION

The Fourteenth Amendment contained the first constitutional definition of citizenship: "All persons born or naturalized in the United States, and subject to the jurisdiction thereof, are citizens of the United States and of the State wherein they reside." This sentence, known as the citizenship clause, undid the *Dred Scott* ruling. Senator Jacob Howard, who introduced the wording, told Congress the sentence "settles the great question of citizenship and removes all doubt as to what persons are or are not citizens of the United States." The words, however, did not settle the question; they set off a debate that continues today.

The controversy is over the phrase "subject to the jurisdiction thereof." The phrase generated considerable debate before it was accepted. It was meant simply to clarify that children born to foreign diplomats while they were in the United States were not U.S. citizens. Some senators suggested the phrase meant "not owing allegiance to anybody else [but the United States]." That interpretation ruled out Native Americans, who owed at least some allegiance to their tribes. The majority thought the expression had to do with being under the rules and protections of U.S. laws, public officials, and judges. By that meaning, almost everyone born in the country, including children of noncitizen immigrants, could be classified as citizens.

BIRTHRIGHT CITIZENSHIP

The citizenship clause established the concept of birthright citizenship: that is, being born in the United States confers the right of citizenship. That concept was tested in 1898 in the case of *United States v. Wong Kim Ark*. Wong, the son of Chinese immigrants to California, had taken a trip to China. When he tried to return home, he was told he could not reenter the country because a law forbade Chinese people from coming to America. Wong protested, insisting that he was a U.S. citizen. The California district court agreed he could not reenter, but the federal government took the matter to the Supreme Court. The justices found that "a child born in the United States, of parents of Chinese descent, who, at the time of his birth, are subjects of the Emperor of China . . . becomes at the time of his birth a citizen of the United States, by virtue of the first clause of the Fourteenth Amendment of the Constitution."

The judges based their decision on English common law, unwritten but well-accepted understandings that had been followed for centuries in England, the

Wong Kim Ark was in his early twenties when he challenged a U.S. Customs official, claiming that his birth on U.S. soil made him a U.S. citizen.

American colonies, and the United States. Under English common law, a person born in a given country is automatically under the jurisdiction of that country. However, the ruling was not unanimous. In his dissent, the chief justice explained that Americans were not bound by all the principles of English common law. In declaring independence from England, he argued, the Founding Fathers rejected the notion that citizenship was forever bound to a person's place of birth. Nevertheless, the majority opinion prevailed: the *Wong Kim Ark* ruling declared that the Fourteenth Amendment granted birthright citizenship.

The issue resurfaced in the 1990s because of the large number of immigrants who were in the country illegally. Many of the immigrants were having children in the United States. Some people accused them of giving birth in America in the hope that having U.S.-born children might increase their chances of becoming legal, or at least avoiding deportation. Some called the children "anchor babies" because these tiny citizens served as anchors keeping their parents in the country. Some politicians proposed new laws stating that children born to people who are not in the country legally are not U.S. citizens. The controversy continues today.

Those who want to change the law base their efforts on a reinterpretation of the citizenship clause. They argue that immigrants who do not have a legal right to be in America are not subject to its jurisdiction. They point out that when the Fourteenth Amendment was written, there was no illegal immigration, and they contend that the birthright citizenship in the amendment cannot be applied to a category of people who did not exist at the time the amendment was approved. Since 1993, various senators and representatives have proposed legislation and some have suggested a constitutional amendment to redefine citizenship. To date, none of those efforts has succeeded.

CHAPTER TWO

RESIDENCY

Citizenship is only half of the immigration issue. The other half concerns residency—that is, who can enter the United States, who can be barred, and who can be removed. The Constitution says nothing about the residency part of immigration. As with citizenship, the events and attitudes of the times shaped the evolving policy on residency.

For sixty years after the Constitution was ratified, no one in the federal government paid much attention to immigration. When immigration caused a problem, the states handled it. The most common problem was the arrival of immigrants who were poor, sick, or guilty of crimes. Some states required the masters of ships bringing immigrants to their shores to pay a tax on each person—a head tax—and report how many were on board.

When one ship's master failed to comply with the tax, New York fined him. The ship's

Once steamships largely replaced sailing ships for ocean travel, immigration rose. These immigrants are arriving in New York on a paddle steamer in 1858.

master argued that the state had no authority to regulate trade with a foreign country. The Supreme Court did not look at the case as a matter of commerce. In *New York v. Miln* (1837), the justices ruled that the state could control who entered its territory because it had "police power," or the responsibility to protect its inhabitants.

IMMIGRATION AS COMMERCE

The states did not retain control over immigration for long. In 1849, two ships' masters challenged similar

laws in Massachusetts and New York. The Supreme
Court combined the cases as the Passenger Cases. The
ships' masters made the same argument as in the previous case: only the federal government, not state
governments, could make rules about trade with other
countries. That authority came from the Constitution's
commerce clause: "The Congress shall have power . . .
to regulate commerce with foreign nations, and
among the several states, and with the Indian tribes."
Regulating commerce is one of the enumerated powers
assigned to Congress in Article I, Section 8.

The justices were asked to decide whether trans-
porting free people from foreign nations constituted
commerce. They also had to examine whether the
Constitution gave Congress the exclusive power to
regulate commerce or allowed the states some authority. After contentious debate, the justices could not
agree. The five-to-four ruling was that states could
not charge the tax.

Because the justices had so many different opinions,
the Passenger Cases did not set a firm foundation for
using the commerce clause as authority for federal
regulation of immigration. A stronger precedent came
with the 1876 *Henderson v. Mayor of New York* decision. The Supreme Court ruled that immigration was
indeed commerce between the United States and foreign nations. Furthermore, the commerce clause gave

Congress and Congress alone the power to make laws governing immigration.

Eight years later, the Court reaffirmed its position after Congress passed a law levying a federal head tax on each immigrant. In its first ruling on an immigration law, the Head Money Cases, the Supreme Court declared that the fee was not a tax but a way to regulate foreign commerce. The early constitutional tie between immigration and commerce is reflected in the fact that when the government created the Bureau of Immigration in 1891, it was a division of the Treasury Department.

AN ISSUE OF SOVEREIGNTY

By the 1880s some Americans had begun to consider certain people coming to the country as a problem. In response, Congress began to enact laws restricting immigration. For example, in 1882, Congress passed the first Chinese Exclusion Act, which forbade the immigration of Chinese workers for ten years. Challenges to the laws led to the establishment of another basis for federal control of immigration.

One important challenge came in the case *Chae Chan Ping v. United States* (1889). Chae Chan Ping had followed all the rules for immigrants. Before he went to China for a visit, he obtained the documents he would need to be readmitted on his return. But while he was away, the government changed the law, saying that no one from China could enter the United States. Chae Chan Ping complained to the courts, asserting that the new law was not valid.

The Supreme Court needed to determine what grounds Congress had for making a law that excluded specific categories of immigrants. The Court found the

SUPREME COURT OF THE UNITED STATES.

The Fuller Court, headed by Chief Justice Melville Fuller, made many important decisions from 1888 to 1910. It was the first to express the doctrine of federal plenary power over immigration.

basis for the law not in an enumerated power specifically cited in the Constitution but in a power that was implied by the Constitution. The justices reasoned that every nation has the right to do certain things to maintain its sovereignty, or independence from the control or influence of other nations. Among those are making treaties, declaring war, raising money—and controlling who can travel past the nation's borders. Since Congress is the governmental branch with the constitutional right to do many of these things, it made sense that Congress would be the federal body to determine who can or cannot enter the country. In another case, *Fong Yue Ting v. United States* (1893), the Court ruled that Congress also had the power to say who could be removed from the country.

Taken together, these two decisions meant that Congress could make whatever immigration laws it wished; the need to protect national sovereignty gave Congress total authority over immigration. Full and complete power over a matter is called plenary power. The rulings in *Chae Chan Ping v. United States* and *Fong Yue Ting v. United States* declared that Congress, together with the executives that carry out the laws Congress makes, had plenary power over immigration.

CONSTITUTIONAL PROVISIONS RELATING TO IMMIGRATION

The Constitution does not address immigration directly, but it does talk about citizenship. Lawmakers and judges have used the following passages to make decisions about immigration issues.

Article I, Section 8: "The Congress shall have power . . . to establish a uniform rule of naturalization."

Article I, Section 8 (Commerce Clause): "The Congress shall have power . . . to regulate commerce with foreign nations, and among the several states, and with the Indian tribes."

Article VI, Clause 2 (Supremacy Clause): "This Constitution, and the Laws of the United States which shall be made in pursuance thereof; and all treaties made, or which shall be made, under the authority of the United States, shall be the supreme law of the land; and the judges in every state shall be bound thereby, anything in the constitution or laws of any state to the contrary notwithstanding."

Amendment XIV, Section 1 (Citizenship, Equal Protection, and Due Process Clauses): "All persons born or naturalized in the United States, and subject to the jurisdiction thereof, are citizens of the

United States and of the State wherein they reside. No State shall make or enforce any law which shall abridge the privileges or immunities of citizens of the United States; nor shall any State deprive any person of life, liberty, or property, without due process of law; nor deny to any person within its jurisdiction the equal protection of the laws."

PLENARY POWER = ABSOLUTE CONTROL

Having plenary power means no other person or body has any say-so in a matter—not even judges. This was clarified in *Nishimura Ekiu v. United States* (1892), also known as the Japanese Immigrant Case. Nishimura Ekiv had been denied admission to the United States and placed in a facility until she could be returned to Japan. She complained that she was being denied her due process rights. Nishimura was referring to nearly identical clauses in the Fifth and Fourteenth Amendments called the due process clauses: "No person shall . . . be deprived of life, liberty, or property, without due process of law." She believed that she was deprived of her liberty without fair legal proceedings. In her case, the Court first restated the doctrine of plenary power:

It is an accepted maxim of international law that every sovereign nation has the power, as inherent in sovereignty and essential to self-preservation, to forbid the entrance of foreigners within its dominions or to admit them . . . as it may see fit.

Then the Court went further. It said no judges needed to examine the laws Congress made about immigration matters because Congress had plenary power in that area. Nishimura was not entitled to any help from the courts. The Supreme Court declared, "As to such persons [foreigners], the decisions of executive or administrative officers, acting within powers expressly conferred by Congress, are due process of law." In other words, whatever action Congress declared and officials carried out regarding foreigners was all the "due process" anyone would get.

Following this case, the courts would long stay silent on issues of immigration. For nearly one hundred years immigrants and would-be immigrants who felt unfairly treated had no recourse.

CHAPTER THREE

THE POWER TO SAY NO

The period from 1820 to 1924 is often called the Century of Immigration. During that time, approximately thirty-six million foreigners came to the United States. In the beginning, they were welcome. The Industrial Revolution had created a tremendous need for workers in American factories. The boom in manufacturing meant there was a great demand for new methods of transportation, and laborers were needed to build canals and lay railroad tracks. American companies advertised overseas for people to fill the many job openings.

As the Civil War took men from the factories to the battlefield, the labor shortage grew worse. The need for foreign workers was so acute that the very first national immigration law was called An Act to Encourage Immigration. The law, passed in 1864, made it easier for immigrants

In the late 1800s, many immigrants, including children, worked in American factories. This child is stoking a coal-burning stove in a shop that manufactures metal goods.

to work immediately upon entering the country, and it exempted them from military service.

REMOVING THE WELCOME MAT

But by the middle of the Century of Immigration, public opinion had shifted. The steady growth in the number of immigrants outpaced the number of jobs. The new arrivals were willing to work for less money than native-born workers, and businesses were happy to employ them. As wages fell and unemployment rose, many people began to resent the immigrants.

Some of the anti-immigrant feeling was also caused by racial and religious prejudice. Predominantly Protestant communities distrusted the mostly Catholic German and Irish immigrants. Californians disliked the Chinese, who poured into their ports and established mining claims in their hills. Some stereotyped Italians as criminals. Others considered anyone from eastern Europe inferior. The prejudice often erupted into violence.

States and cities enacted regulations against immigrants, particularly the Chinese. Chinese in California had to pay a foreign miners' tax. They could not testify in court, and their children were barred from public schools. In San Francisco, Chinese immigrants could not wear their hair in braids and could not carry objects in the traditional way. The California legislature passed an "anti-coolie" act in 1862 that required people of Chinese origin to pay a monthly tax to operate any business. (The term "coolie," which originally meant a Chinese laborer who worked under contract, became a slanderous word for any Asian worker.) The official title of the legislation illustrates

THE CHANGING FOCUS OF IMMIGRATION SERVICES

The history of the federal agencies that have regulated immigration reveals changes in the country's concerns about immigration: from its cost to its impact on the workforce to law enforcement to national security.

1891 The Office of Superintendent of Immigration (later the Bureau of Immigration) is established under the **Department of the Treasury**.

1903 The Bureau of Immigration is moved to the newly created **Department of Commerce and Labor**.

1913 The Department of Commerce and Labor is split into separate departments, and the Bureau of Immigration is placed under the **Department of Labor**.

1933 The Bureaus of Immigration and Naturalization are merged to create the Immigration and Naturalization Service (INS).

1940 The INS is moved from the Department of Labor to the **Department of Justice**.

2003 The INS is dissolved and its functions divided among three agencies under the **Department of Homeland Security**: the United States Citizenship and Immigration Service, Immigration and Customs Enforcement (ICE), and Customs and Border Patrol.

the sentiment of many in the state at the time: An Act to Protect Free White Labor Against Competition with Chinese Coolie Labor, and to Discourage the Immigration of the Chinese into the State of California.

SLAMMING THE DOOR ON ASIANS

For some people, discouraging immigration of the Chinese was not enough; they wanted to forbid it entirely. An anti-immigrant movement called nativism arose, and its adherents began to clamor for laws against immigration and immigrants. Nativist groups believed America belonged to the descendants of the thirteen original colonies. They pushed for national restriction of all immigration. Their first victory was against the Chinese.

The first federal immigration law, the Page Act (1875), prohibited three groups of people from entering the United States: those who were convicts in their home countries, Asian males engaged in forced labor, and Asian women who were prostitutes. Immigration officials assumed all Chinese laborers were engaged in forced labor, and they treated nearly all the Chinese women seeking to immigrate as likely prostitutes. Therefore the law kept out most Chinese. But that was not sufficient for some nativists. They continued to pressure Congress to stop Chinese immigration completely.

Barring Chinese immigrants was not easy because the Burlingame Treaty had given the Chinese "free migration" to the United States. To get around this barrier, an amendment to the treaty was negotiated in 1880. The amended arrangement allowed the United States to "regulate, limit, or suspend" but "not absolutely prohibit" immigration of Chinese laborers. This was the loophole Congress needed to pass the Chinese Exclusion Act (1882). The legislation provided that for ten years "the coming of Chinese laborers to the United States" would be suspended. Technically this law, which amounted to the complete and total exclusion of immigration from China, did not violate the terms of the treaty. When the ten-year term ran out in 1892, the Geary Act extended the provisions for another ten years. When that act expired in 1902, they were again extended, this time indefinitely.

Although the Chinese were the most obvious targets of anti-immigrant legislation, they were not the only ones. Through the Gentlemen's Agreement (1907) between Japan and the United States, Japanese immigration was also severely curtailed. What had once been called the Golden Door—the gateway to the land of the free—was virtually slammed shut to all Asians.

[Public No. 71]

Forty-seventh

Congress of the United States, At the First Session,

Begun and held at the CITY OF WASHINGTON, in the DISTRICT OF COLUMBIA, on Monday, the *fifth* day of *December*, eighteen hundred and eighty-*one*

An Act

To execute certain treaty stipulations relating to Chinese.

Whereas, In the opinion of the Government of the United States the coming of Chinese laborers to this country endangers the good order of certain localities within the territory thereof: Therefore, *Be it enacted by the Senate and House of Representatives of the United States of America in Congress assembled,* That from and after the expiration of ninety days next after the passage of this act, and until the expiration of ten years next after the passage of this act, the coming of Chinese laborers to the United States be, and the same is hereby, suspended; and during such suspension it shall not be lawful for any Chinese laborer to come, or, having so come after the expiration of said ninety days, to remain within the United States.

Sec. 2. That the master of any vessel who shall knowingly bring within the United States on such vessel, and land or permit to be landed, any Chinese laborer, from any foreign port or place, shall be deemed guilty of a misdemeanor, and on conviction thereof shall be punished by a fine of not more than five hundred dollars for each and every such Chinese laborer so brought, and may be also imprisoned for a term not exceeding one year.

Sec. 3. That the two foregoing sections shall not apply to Chinese laborers who were in the United States on the seventeenth day of November, eighteen hundred and eighty, or who shall have come into the same before the expiration of ninety days next after the passage of this act, and who shall produce

As this first page of the Chinese Exclusion Act states, anyone bringing Chinese people to the United States could be fined $500 per person and imprisoned for a year.

SEALING THE CRACKS

All that remained to end the Century of Immigration was to seal any cracks in the door—a goal that was accomplished by the courts.

Thousands of Asians who were denied admission or deported challenged those actions. But time and again the courts upheld the decisions of customs agents. *Chae Chan Ping v. United States* and *Yue Ting v. United States* set the precedents. In these cases, the Supreme Court ruled that the Chinese Exclusion Act and later legislation that supported exclusion of Asians were perfectly constitutional. Congress and its agents had plenary power to decide who could be admitted to the country and who could be removed.

Asians who came to the United States before the door was shut generally did not have to fear deportation. But they had no hope of becoming American citizens. Although a naturalization law passed in 1870 extended citizenship to African Americans, Asians remained under the definitions of the 1790 law, which reserved naturalization for "free white persons."

Did that mean that Asians could not claim any of the protections listed in the Constitution? The Fourteenth Amendment promises, "No State shall . . . deny to any person within its jurisdiction the equal protection of the laws." This provision is known as the equal protection clause. Did it apply to noncitizens or only to citizens? Immigrants were sometimes mistreated; did they have any legal way to fight the discrimination? Did mere residency in the United States give them the same protections as citizens?

RIGHTS OF RESIDENCY

Yes, the Supreme Court decided, first in the case of *Yick Wo v. Hopkins* (1886). Yick Wo had a laundry business in San Francisco. The city enacted an ordinance requiring anyone operating a laundry in a wooden building to obtain a permit from the Board of Supervisors. Of the 310 laundries in San Francisco in wooden buildings, 240 had Chinese operators. When people applied for the permits, all but one non-Chinese operator received them, but every Chinese laundry owner was refused. Yick Wo had a license that was still valid, so he continued to operate his business. He was fined for not having a permit. When he refused to pay the fine, he was put in jail. He appealed to the judicial system.

In a unanimous decision, the justices ruled that although nothing was wrong with the ordinance itself, the way the city enforced the law discriminated

When Chinese immigrants in California were ousted from their mining claims, they started laundries, restaurants, and grocery businesses to make money from the miners.

unfairly. The opinion said Yick Wo, even though he was not a citizen, could not be treated differently from non-Chinese people:

> The Fourteenth Amendment to the Constitution is not confined to the protection of citizens. . . . [Its] provisions are universal in their application, to all persons within the territorial jurisdiction, without regard to any differences of race, of color, or of nationality.

This ruling was a landmark decision, an opinion that changed the way courts viewed the principle of equal protection.

In the Slaughterhouse Cases decided thirteen years earlier, the first important test of the then five-year-old Fourteenth Amendment, a sharply divided Supreme Court had offered a different understanding of the amendment. In its 1873 decision, the Court distinguished between the "privileges and immunities" belonging to citizens of the country and those belonging to citizens of a state. The Court ruled that the Fourteenth Amendment protected only those rights specifically named in or implied by the Constitution as belonging to U.S. citizens. The states were responsible for seeing that people received whatever rights and protections the state defined for its citizens.

The *Yick Wo* decision rejected that narrow interpretation, which suggested that the Fourteenth Amendment did not protect noncitizens at all. Instead, the Court declared that the amendment protected the rights of all inhabitants of the country equally, regardless of citizenship status.

Other cases followed that reinforced the new understanding. The *Yick Wo* case set a precedent that would be cited in more than 160 cases dealing with civil rights. After *Yick Wo*, aliens were able to enjoy the same privileges and immunities as citizens with the exception of voting and holding federal office.

CHAPTER FOUR

A POLICY TAKES SHAPE

n its first hundred years, the United States had no real immigration policy. Borders were open, and the only action Congress took was to forbid entry to convicts and the Chinese. But as the twentieth century dawned, public sentiment increasingly turned against immigrants. Political, social, and economic upheavals in many parts of the globe had spawned mass exoduses of people, thousands of whom had made their way to America. Many were poor, uneducated, and unskilled. The general perception was that they brought disease, crime, and crowded conditions to the nation's cities. A severe economic depression in the 1890s made matters worse.

As anti-immigrant fervor mounted, a policy began to emerge to exclude people considered "undesirable." A series of laws from 1882 to 1901 denied entry to convicts, lunatics, paupers, polygamists, people with infectious diseases,

Judge.]

THE EVILS OF UNRESTRICTED IMMIGRATI

In this 1891 cartoon, which reflected the country's mood on immigration, immigrants are blamed for bringing the Mafia, anarchism, socialism, and other "evils" to the United States.

[March 28, 1891.

political extremists, and Chinese and Japanese people. Immigration had become a political flashpoint, and Congress created a bipartisan commission to study the issue and make recommendations for addressing it.

The Dillingham Commission was charged with investigating "the sources of recent immigration . . . the general character of incoming immigrants . . . and the effect of such immigration upon the institutions, industries, and people of this country." The nine members of the commission worked for four years, from 1907 to 1911, and produced forty-two volumes of statistical information. They concluded that the "new immigrants," those who arrived after 1883, were quite different from the old ones. Most of the early immigrants had come from western Europe.

According to the commission, this group of immigrants was resourceful, hardworking, and dedicated to being part of their new homeland. Of the recent immigrants, however, more than 70 percent were from southern and eastern Europe. The commissioners pronounced the new immigrants less progressive, "far less intelligent," more transient, and unwilling to assimilate.

The commissioners may have been influenced by the eugenics movement, which was popular at the time. Eugenics, which reached its peak in the Nazi pursuit of the "Master Race," held that some races were superior to others physically, intellectually, and culturally. In the view of the Dillingham Commission, people from eastern and southern Europe were inferior to native-born citizens, most of whom were descended from western Europeans. The presence of so many new immigrants posed a danger to American society and culture. The commission recommended severely restricting their ability to enter the country. Congress found ways to do that through the Immigration Act of 1917.

DISCRIMINATING INDIRECTLY

Rather than bar people from specific countries, Congress chose to use two criteria for entry that it thought would accomplish the same purpose: literacy and the ability to pay a tax. The first provision of the Immigration Act raised the head tax on adult immigrants from four dollars to eight dollars. That amount may seem small, but it was enough to keep many families from attempting to come to America. Another section banned a number of categories of immigrants who were likely to require financial support.

The Dillingham Commission had recommended a literacy test as the best way to keep out the "undesirables." Requiring would-be immigrants to show they could read had been tried before, but three different presidents had vetoed the earlier bills. Congress tried again, stating that in order to enter the United States, aliens over the age of sixteen had to be able to read thirty to forty words in any language they chose. President Woodrow Wilson rejected the bill, but this time Congress overrode his veto.

The congressmen did not feel the need to be indirect in barring Asians. The Chinese and Japanese were already excluded, but the framers of the law wanted to keep out all Asians. They created an Asiatic Barred Zone, which encompassed nearly all the lands and islands of Asia and the Middle East. No one from this zone could get into America.

BORDER PATROL

The people coming to the United States across the Rio Grande in 1904 were not Mexican; most were Chinese. The Immigration Service had few people to stop them. From a single station in El Paso, Texas, seventy-five guards patrolled all the way to California on horseback. A decade later, more stations were added, and some of the guards had cars. Sometimes the army or the Texas Rangers helped.

The drastic restrictions on immigration in the 1920s brought more people to the unguarded spaces between inspection stations. To keep them out, Congress created the U.S. Border Patrol in 1924. The first agents had little in the way of equipment: each was issued a single revolver. They did not even have uniforms, but their badges identified them as federal agents. They had to supply their own horses and saddles, but the agency fed the horses.

Over the years, the Border Patrol's equipment became much more sophisticated: planes, helicopters, infrared night-vision scopes, and seismic sensors. The agency is currently talking about using unmanned drones.

Today's Border Patrol agents look very different from the lone horsemen of ninety years ago. Although some still ride horses, others use all-terrain motorcycles, bicycles, boats, and snowmobiles. They patrol 6,000 miles (9,656 kilometers) of land

Four men trying to enter the United States illegally in 1947 are stopped and searched by Border Patrol agents before being sent back across the border to Mexico.

along the borders with Mexico and Canada and 2,000 miles (3,219 km) of coast surrounding Florida and Puerto Rico. According to CPB.gov, their primary mission is "to detect and prevent the illegal entry of aliens" and "protect our nation by reducing the likelihood that dangerous people and capabilities enter the United States."

A NUMBERS GAME

The 1917 law did little to slow immigration. Newcomers continued to arrive, and fear of foreigners mushroomed. World War I and the Bolshevik Revolution sent thousands fleeing Europe and Russia for the safety and freedom of America. The mood in the United States was one of isolation. People did not want to be involved in the turmoil going on overseas, and they certainly did not want that turmoil coming to U.S. shores. A frenzy called the Red Scare gripped the nation, convincing many that Communists were hatching plots that would cause chaos. In a climate of widespread unemployment and heightened nationalism, newspapers were full of warnings about the dangers of the "new" immigrants.

Congress calmed the hysteria somewhat with the Emergency Quota Act of 1921. The act marked a turning point in immigration legislation. It introduced numbers into the discussion and imposed greater government control. Rather than allowing anyone into the country who was not specifically excluded, Congress would dictate the number of immigrants who would be permitted to enter. Furthermore, Congress would decide how many would be admitted from any one country.

This 1921 cartoon uses the image of a giant funnel, narrowed at the end by Uncle Sam, to illustrate the Emergency Quota Act's severe restriction of emigration from Europe. The papers in his hand represent the new law.

The numbers were set according to a quota system. The number of immigrants from each country was limited to a figure that was 3 percent of a base number. The base was the "number of foreign-born persons of such nationality resident in the United States as determined by the United States census of 1910." The year 1910 was selected as the base year because the large influx of new immigrants did not begin until after that date. Use of this formula effectively barred immigration from southern and eastern Europe. Asians remained excluded, but immigration from the Western Hemisphere was not restricted.

The Emergency Quota Act was supposed to be only temporary, but Congress liked this first major restriction of immigration. Most congressmen wanted to make the restrictions permanent and more stringent. They focused on making the formula more effective at reducing the number of undesired immigrants.

The result was the Johnson-Reed Act, also called the National Origins Act of 1924. The new legislation made two major changes to the formula: the quota was dropped from 3 percent to 2 percent, and the base year was pushed back to 1890. Prior to 1890, the vast majority of foreigners coming to America were from western Europe; very few were from

Poland, Italy, or other nations of eastern or southern Europe. Basing the quota on the 1890 census meant that 70 percent of the available slots went to just three countries: Great Britain, Ireland, and Germany.

The law had the intended effect: immigration from eastern and southern Europe skidded to a standstill. The year 1924 marked the end of the Century of Immigration. It also clarified the country's immigration policy. Using its plenary power, Congress would allow only a trickle of immigrants from outside the Western Hemisphere, and most of them would be western Europeans. This very tight policy and the quota system that defined it remained in effect for forty-one years.

CHAPTER FIVE

THE POLICY LOOSENS A BIT

The lull in immigration after the passage of the National Origins Act was followed by the Great Depression. America's factories offered no work that would draw immigrants. But when the United States entered World War II, new political and economic realities called for changes in immigration policy.

The war altered America's relationship with China. When China entered the conflict on the side of the Allies, the exclusion of Chinese immigrants became an embarrassment to the United States. Thirteen thousand Chinese fought in the war in American uniforms. For the sake of good relations with a wartime ally, Congress passed the Magnuson Act (1943), repealing the Chinese exclusion laws and allowing Chinese immigrants to become naturalized citizens.

The Magnuson Act made little real difference in the immigration numbers, as it set the quota for Chinese immigrants at 105 a year. But it did begin a loosening of the restrictive immigration policy. Two years later, immigration and naturalization barriers against Filipinos and people from India were also removed.

GUESTS INVITED

World War II created a labor shortage as men left their farms and factories to fight. The shortage was particularly acute in agriculture and on the railroads. Americans had always looked to immigrants when they needed laborers. This time they looked to Mexico. The United States and Mexico agreed to allow thousands of Mexicans to work in the United States on a temporary basis. The Mexicans would be guest workers, known as braceros. They would have contracts spelling out the conditions under which they would work, and they would have certain guarantees and protections.

When a guest worker's contract ended, he could apply for another. But he would have to go back to Mexico, wait his turn, deal with red tape and fees, and possibly pay bribes. Many chose to simply stay in the United States and work without a contract. And many employers were more than happy to hire them. The

Braceros arriving in Stockton, California, in 1943 hold American and Mexican flags and make V's with their fingers to signal working together for victory in World War II.

bracero then became an illegal immigrant, but neither he nor his employer suffered any penalties. American growers were so eager to keep the low-wage aliens that they encouraged the illegal stays. Arresting agents took the illegal immigrants to the border, fast-tracked them in getting a new contract, and brought them back as legal guest workers. They remained legal until the contract ran out— and then they began the process again.

The presence of guest workers fostered conditions that promoted future illegal immigration from Mexico. It enabled the agriculture industry to expand, requiring more workers. Braceros, who usually worked seasonally and returned year after year, formed contacts that helped them find jobs and housing in the United States. The money they brought to

FROM GUEST TO CITIZEN

At sixteen years of age, Heriberto Lugo had been helping his father with farm work for years, according to the Bracero History Archive, a project of the Center for History and New Media. When he was fifteen, he had to quit school to work full-time in the fields. He saw braceros returning to Mexico from their jobs in the United States with good clothes, sturdy shoes, and other niceties, things no one else in his little town even dreamed of having. Lugo decided to see for himself what life and work "in the north" was like.

Instead of going through the guest worker program, Lugo simply came across the border. Once across, he had no trouble finding a job; work in the beet, alfalfa, and tomato fields of California was plentiful for strong, young Mexicans in 1952.

The work was also hard. In his first days, bent over while topping beets in the hot sun, Lugo thought he would die from exhaustion. But he stuck it out. When immigration agents took him back to Mexico, Lugo returned over and over to the farms in California. In the off-season he cut and sold firewood.

After two years as an undocumented alien, Lugo applied for a bracero contract. He worked for four years at a farm labor camp with four to five hundred other braceros. In addition to pay for his work, he received food, housing, and clothing. Every month he sent money home to his father.

A Mexican bracero picks carrots and ties them into bunches on a U.S. farm in the 1950s. His only protections from the elements are kneepads and a wide-brimmed hat.

At the end of his fourth year as a bracero, Lugo filed the necessary paperwork and received permission to immigrate to the United States not as a guest but as a permanent resident. He had demonstrated good character and a willingness to work hard—the stuff good citizens are made of.

their villages made some in Mexico dependent on having citizens employed in the United States. The flooding of the farm labor market with large numbers of aliens drove native workers to other industries, creating the need for even more farm workers.

The long-term use of what was supposed to be a temporary solution to a short-term problem had unintended consequences. No one expected the program to last beyond the war. But the bracero program was anything but temporary. The Korean conflict and grower demands resulted in several extensions that kept it in place for twenty-one years.

HOME FOR THE HOMELESS

While Mexicans were crossing the border with relative ease, another group was begging to come into the United States. They were the thousands who had survived persecution during World War II. Most had their homes taken from them or destroyed. Many could not return to their cities, where discrimination was still harsh. They were displaced persons—people with nowhere to go. But the strict quotas of U.S. immigration policy kept out all but a few.

President Truman tried to get Congress to work around the quotas and admit some of the nearly two million displaced persons. But Congress was discussing bills that would make the quotas even smaller. Most of the refugees from the war were from eastern Europe, and many were Jews; prejudice against both groups was strong in the United States at the time. But individuals and citizen groups pressured Congress to do something about the suffering of so many, and Congress passed a displaced persons bill in 1948.

These are among the 641 refugees that arrived in New York from Germany in November 1947 aboard the SS *Ernie Pyle*. In their suitcases are all the possessions they own.

The law did not do away with the quotas. It permitted two hundred thousand displaced persons to come to America over two years. However, their numbers would be counted against quotas for future years. In other words, more than the quota amounts could come in for two years, but for many years thereafter no one from those countries would be able to immigrate because the countries' quotas were reached. The law also specified exactly which refugee groups could apply for admittance; the lines were drawn in a way that excluded many Jews.

Congress presented the bill to President Truman on the last day of its session before retiring for the summer break. Truman was furious. He called the bill "flagrantly discriminatory." The president's only options were to sign the bill or wait for Congress to return and try to negotiate a better arrangement. He had been trying for three years to talk Congress into more compassionate legislation. With "very great reluctance," he signed the bill into law.

As deeply flawed as Truman and others considered the act, it did loosen immigration policy a bit. After two years it was amended, permitting a total of four hundred thousand displaced persons to enter the country. In addition, it granted admittance to three thousand orphaned refugees outside the quota system.

It was a small number, but it was a relaxation in the quota system.

A LOPSIDED COMPROMISE

The Displaced Persons Act recognized a new category of immigrant: the refugee. This category did not fit easily into immigration law with its emphasis on different countries and ethnic groups. Therefore, a debate began on restructuring the law. On one side of the debate were "restrictionists," who wanted to make getting into America even more difficult. On the other side were "liberals," who wanted to admit more people.

The restrictionists saw immigration policy as an issue of national security. They were nativists, or people who thought that keeping out foreigners was the best way to make America safe. The liberals saw immigration as a matter of foreign policy. They were internationalists who believed that generous immigration practices would make for friendly relations with other nations and establish the United States as a leader in world freedom. The debate ended with a restrictive law passed over the veto of President Truman: the Immigration and Nationality Act (1952), also known as the McCarran-Walter Act.

The first group of people to come to the United States under the Displaced Persons Act traveled on a U.S. Army transport in 1948. On board were 813 people from eleven countries.

The new law maintained the quotas based on national origin. It barred anyone who might undermine the government and its laws, such as Communists, and called for their immediate deportation. It removed some of the barriers to Asian immigration and naturalization but kept quotas for Asians very low. Because the number of applications far exceeded the number of quota slots, the law established a priority system. Preference was given first to applicants with specific skills that were needed in America, and then to those with family already in the United States. No quotas were imposed on immigration from any country in the Western Hemisphere.

The law made one concession to the liberals. It gave non-quota status to spouses of American citizens, enabling husbands as well as wives to enter without being subject to quota restrictions. This was only a slight relaxation of immigration policy in a largely restrictive law. However, one provision in the McCarran-Walter Act gave the executive branch a new power regarding immigration, unintentionally opening the door for thousands of people to come to America.

CHAPTER SIX

THE POLICY TIPS TOWARD ALIENS

ection 212 of the McCarran-Walter Act stated that the attorney general "may . . . in his discretion parole into the United States temporarily . . . any alien applying for admission to the United States." Parole power was to be used "only on a case-by-case basis for urgent humanitarian reasons or significant public benefit." Paroled aliens are not technically admitted to the United States; they are simply allowed to live in the country for a time. Once the urgency is over, they are supposed to go back to their home countries.

The constitutional basis for parole power is the plenary power doctrine: Congress has the right to make any laws about immigration it sees fit. Officials of the executive branch carry out the laws, but the courts do not rule on their constitutionality. The judiciary is hands-off because all power—that is what "plenary" means—for immigration law is vested in Congress.

The absolute right of the executive branch to use parole was affirmed in the case *Shaughnessy v. Mezei* (1953). The attorney general had denied a resident alien reentry to the United States because he was a security risk. Immigration officials kept him on Ellis Island while he made arrangements for where he would go. He applied to several countries, but none would let him in. After twenty-one months, the district court granted him parole—permission to live in the United States rather than on Ellis Island—while he continued to look for a permanent home. The Supreme Court reversed the lower court's action, cancelling the parole. The justices explained, "The alien's right to enter the United States depends on the congressional will, and the courts cannot substitute their judgment for the legislative mandate." In other words, all decisions regarding admission or denial of admission to the country, including parole decisions, belong exclusively to Congress and the executives who carry out Congress's will.

MERCY TRUMPS QUOTAS

The framers of the McCarran-Walter Act envisioned parole power being used very rarely and only for hardship cases. It was not meant to be applied to entire categories of people. However, the first president

After the Soviet army brutally crushed the 1956 Hungarian rebellion, refugees from Hungary waited near the border with Austria for some country to take them in.

to take office after the law was enacted used the power to bring a large group to the United States. At the time, thousands in Europe were without homes, still recovering from the devastation of war, and thousands more were fleeing Communist oppression. Restrictionist sentiment was still strong, but a growing number of Americans were moved by the plight of Europe's refugees. President Dwight D. Eisenhower encouraged Congress to pass the Refugee Relief Act (1953). This emergency legislation authorized visas outside the quota system to 205,000 people who lacked "the essentials of life."

Three years later, a student demonstration in Hungary escalated into a full-scale revolt against Communist rule. The uprising was brutally crushed, and two hundred thousand escaped to Austria. They could not all stay in Austria, but they faced certain death if they returned to Hungary. Eisenhower saw their need as a humanitarian crisis and an opportunity to stand against Communism. Congress, however, did not want to admit more people from Hungary than the 865 allotted by the quota system. Over the objections of many congressmen, the president used his parole power to bring forty thousand Hungarian refugees to America. Once they were in the country, Congress passed the Hungarian Escape Act (1958) to give them official refugee status.

Other presidents have relied on parole power in other humanitarian emergencies. Presidents Kennedy, Johnson, Ford, Carter, Clinton, and Obama admitted refugees from Cuba, Southeast Asia, and Haiti. Usually when large groups are paroled into the United States, Congress enacts legislation after the fact that gives the parolees some type of legal residency status.

According to the McCarran-Walter Act, parole power can also be used to achieve "significant public benefit." President Barack Obama applied this principle in 2010 when he implemented a policy called "parole in place" for immediate family members of U.S. citizens serving in the military. The policy allows undocumented spouses, parents, and children of U.S. military personnel to go through the process of becoming legal residents without leaving the country.

RESTRICTIONS LIFT

The result of so many exceptions to the quota rules was that in every year McCarran-Walter was in effect, more non-quota aliens than quota aliens came to the United States. The quota system was obviously not working. Besides, Congress was less concerned with certain types of immigrants threatening American culture than with America being a world leader. Immigration had become more about foreign policy

WET FEET OR DRY?

In the early 1990s, immigration from Cuba began to spike. President Bill Clinton feared a repeat of some of the disasters of the mass immigration from Cuba that had occurred decades earlier. Many had died in the dangerous attempt to cross the 90 miles (145 km) from the island nation in leaky, makeshift vessels. The president made an agreement with Cuba that would discourage Cubans from trying to come to America. Part of that agreement was a "wet foot, dry foot" policy. If U.S. authorities intercepted Cubans at sea—that is, with "wet feet"— they would send them back to Cuba. If a Cuban made it past the authorities and landed on American soil— presumably with "dry feet"—that person could stay.

When the U.S. Coast Guard found six Cubans on a raft near Miami, Carlos Hernandez (*left*) jumped into the water and swam to shore. Legally, he was the only one with "dry feet."

than domestic fears. So the entire system of national origins quotas was scrapped. The Hart-Celler Immigration and Nationality Act (1965) replaced it.

The new legislation marked a huge change in policy after more than thirty years of restrictive rules. It set limits on the number of immigrants by hemisphere (Eastern and Western) instead of by country. Preference was given to aliens with ties to U.S. citizens and residents and to those with certain skills. Legally admitted immigrants could bring their family members into the country without those individuals counting toward the hemisphere quota. Eliminating country quotas made room for more immigrants from Latin America and Asia.

COURTS LOOK MORE CLOSELY

The Hart-Celler Act opened the gate for a steady stream of new immigration. The new arrivals created challenges that helped refine immigration law. One of the challenges had to do with deportations. Immigration law permits agents not only to exclude people from entering the country but also to remove, or deport, people who violate the conditions of admission. The government can hold a person who is to be deported until the removal can be arranged.

The case of *Zadvydas v. Davis* (2001) involved a resident alien who was to be deported because he had committed serious crimes. Because no country would take him, it looked like Zadvydas would be held in government detention indefinitely. He appealed to the Supreme Court. The justices would not rule on the constitutionality of the law because the plenary power doctrine kept the judiciary from doing so. But the justices did look at how the executive branch carried out the law. Did its execution of the law deprive Zadvydas of his liberty without "due process," or fair treatment? In the past, the Court had ruled that whatever the executive branch did in enforcing immigration law *was* due process. This time, however, the justices decided that the reason the law permitted aliens to be detained was to work out the deportation. If the deportation could not be arranged, the alien could not be detained. Zadvydas had to be released. The Court was beginning to consider whether an immigrant's rights sometimes temper the doctrine of plenary power.

ILLEGAL IMMIGRANTS ENTER THE EQUATION

One of the biggest factors in the conflict between government power and immigrant rights was the rising tide of illegal aliens. In the late twentieth century, several

According to the Supreme Court's decision in *Plyler v. Doe*, illegal immigrant children are guaranteed the right to a quality and free education in U.S. public schools.

states struggled to provide services for rapidly growing populations. Texas refused to spend state funds to educate children whose parents were not legal residents. The matter reached the Supreme Court, which ruled in *Plyler v. Doe* (1982) that barring the children of illegal aliens from receiving a public education deprived them of the Fourteenth Amendment right of equal protection. Texas attorneys had argued that people who were in the country illegally were not "within its jurisdiction" and therefore not entitled to Fourteenth Amendment rights. The Court disagreed, hearkening back to the *Yick Wo* decision. The justices ruled, "The protection of the Fourteenth Amendment extends to anyone, citizen or stranger, who is subject to the laws of a State." Immigration status was irrelevant; every person physically present in any state, legal or illegal, was entitled to the same rights. The only rights illegal aliens could not claim were those specifically reserved for citizens: the rights to vote and to hold federal office.

Texas's attempt to bar the children of illegal aliens from its schools was a symptom of a larger problem. Throughout the country and particularly in the states along the southern border, the illegal population was swelling. Many people pressured the government to do something to stop the flow. Congress set up the Select Commission on Immigration and Refugee Policy. After five years of study, debate, and compromise, Congress emerged with the Immigration Reform and Control Act, also called the Simpson-Mazzoli Act after the coauthors of the legislation.

A "ONCE AND FOR ALL" REFORM

The 1986 act was heralded as comprehensive immigration reform. Republican senator Alan K. Simpson and Democratic representative Romano L. Mazzoli called the law a "three-legged stool." All three of its main components had to be implemented for the whole law to work. The first leg was keeping people from coming into the

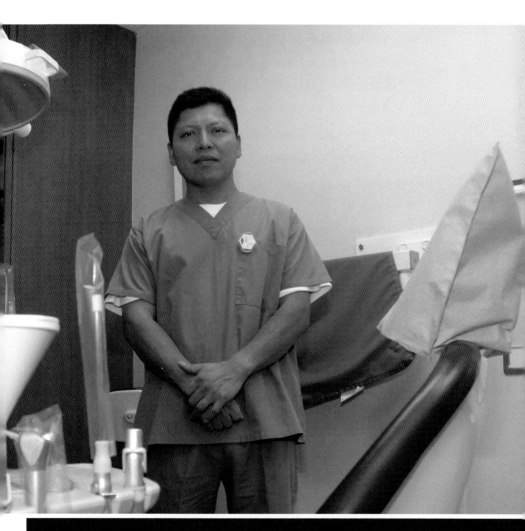

Jose Ortiz came to the United States illegally as a child to escape civil war in El Salvador. Granted amnesty in 1986 under the Simpson-Mazzoli Act, he is now a registered dental assistant and a U.S. citizen.

country illegally. The law put more guards along the borders and tried to remove the main incentive for illegal immigration. It made hiring illegal aliens a crime. Employers had to document the immigration status of their workers and pay stiff penalties if they hired anyone not authorized to be in the United States.

Farmers wanted to keep their cheap labor, so the second leg was a provision that permitted growers to hire foreign agricultural workers on temporary bases. The secretary of labor had to verify that there was a need and that the imported laborers would not affect the wages of those already in the country. Without this provision, congressmen from states that depended on low-cost farm labor would not have voted for the law.

The third leg was quite controversial. Called "status adjustment," it legalized more than three million people who had lived and worked illegally in the country for the previous five years. It granted them amnesty, or forgiveness of the illegal act of entering the country, and enabled them to apply for permanent residency and eventual citizenship. Some people objected to this portion of the legislation, but no one could deny that Congress had absolute power to adjust the residency and citizenship status of anyone as it saw fit.

Nor could critics and supporters deny another glaring fact: Simpson-Mazzoli didn't work. The border security measures were not effective; the additional guards were not sufficient to deal with the numbers of people attempting to slip into the country. The restrictions against hiring illegal aliens were not strong enough or clear enough to keep people from finding ways around them. The flow of illegal immigrants did not stop.

Over the next three decades immigration reforms were made that improved border security and enforcement of existing laws. But the number of people making their way into the United States without authorization continued to climb.

CHAPTER SEVEN

A FOCUS ON ILLEGAL IMMIGRANTS

The costs of illegal immigration fell increasingly on the states. Expenses for jailing criminals and providing education, health care, welfare, and public services rose steeply and steadily. Of course the legal population contributed to the costs, but some citizens believed they had a right to the services whereas people who had broken the law to come to the country did not. Despite the fact that many of the illegal immigrants paid taxes, "natives" often felt they were footing the bill for benefits others received for free.

Congress responded to the states' concerns by toughening some immigration measures. The Illegal Immigration Reform and Immigrant Responsibility Act (1996) placed stiff penalties on alien smuggling, the use of false documents, and other criminal acts. It mandated stricter enforcement of sanctions against employers who hired undocumented workers and barred some illegal immigrants from receiving government benefits.

To put a human face on the issue of deportation, protesters outside an immigration court in Chicago hold photos of the families of the illegal immigrants affected.

Congress recognized that the welfare system that gave financial assistance to legal and illegal alike was one of the magnets that attracted the illegal aliens. It enacted the Personal Responsibility and Work Opportunity Reconciliation Act (1996), making work a requirement of receiving financial aid and capping how long anyone could receive benefits. The new laws helped somewhat, but states wanted more relief.

CALIFORNIA PROPOSITION DEAD IN THE WATER

California sought relief, passing Proposition 187 in 1994 with overwhelming public support. The measure denied health care, education, and welfare benefits to people who were not legally authorized to be in the United States. It required teachers, health care providers, and social workers to report people seeking those benefits to federal authorities.

The day after the proposition passed, several organizations filed lawsuits against it. A federal judge halted implementation until the complaints were resolved. The basis for the block was the *Plyler v. Doe* decision, which established that education was a right guaranteed by the Fourteenth Amendment to all persons "within the jurisdiction" of a state. That covered only one of the issues related to the proposition.

The arguments about the rest dragged on for three years and ended in the Ninth Circuit Court of Appeals in 1997. By that time, the Personal Responsibility Act had become law. That law established guidelines that spelled out how aliens were to receive welfare benefits and required states to follow those guidelines. The rules California set were different from the federal guidelines.

When a state law conflicts with a federal law, the federal law preempts, or trumps, the state law; the federal law stands and the state law is invalid. Preemption is based on the supremacy clause (Article VI, Section 2) of the Constitution:

> This Constitution, and the Laws of the United States which shall be made in pursuance thereof; and all treaties made, or which shall be made, under the authority of the United States, shall be the supreme law of the land; and the judges in every state shall be bound thereby, anything in the constitution or laws of any state to the contrary notwithstanding.

The provisions of Proposition 187 violated the supremacy clause and were therefore preempted.

MANDATORY DETENTION

Soon after the Proposition 187 battle, the terrorist attacks of September 11, 2001, turned the focus of the immigration discussion from costs to security. How had terrorists been able to enter the country? How many more were trying to come in? Could they be kept out? The PATRIOT Act (2001) beefed up border security significantly and made intelligence information about foreigners available to immigration authorities.

Article IV of the PATRIOT Act required federal officials to detain aliens with suspected ties to terrorism and hold them as long as there was reason to believe they may be "engaged in any . . . activity that endangers the security of the United States." That

Immigration officials detained Algerian national Benemar Benatta the day after the terrorist attacks of September 11, 2001. He was held for five years as a potential suspect or witness before finally being released.

means that if they could not be deported, they could be held indefinitely. Critics of the legislation argued that indefinite detention was against the *Zadvydas v. Davis* ruling. They said it violated aliens' right to due process because the government did not have to prove in court that the aliens were threats. Proponents of the legislation countered that detained aliens could have their detention reviewed by the attorney general every six months, and that this was adequate due process. Thousands of aliens have been removed or detained under this law.

The vast majority of people who crossed the border without documents were not terrorists or criminals. Nevertheless, they were breaking the law of the land, and they continued to come. State governors accused the federal government of not enforcing its laws. Some states decided to take matters into their own hands.

ARIZONA TAKES A STAND

One of those states was Arizona. Federal law prohibits employers from knowingly hiring an "unauthorized alien," but employers in Arizona were hiring them anyway, and the federal government was not stopping them. Arizona could not levy fines on employers who broke the federal law because doing so would preempt the federal law that specified its own penalties.

However, the federal law specifically allowed states to regulate licensing of companies. So the Legal Arizona Workers Act (2007) revoked the licenses of employers who hired undocumented workers. The law also required employers to use E-Verify, a system that enabled them to confirm the immigration status of people they wanted to hire.

Businesses and civil rights groups challenged the law. They argued that because the federal government imposed sanctions on employers, the state could not. However, the Supreme Court ruled in *Chamber of Commerce v. Whiting* (2011) that the federal law did not preempt the revoking of licenses. The first battle was a win for the state.

Arizona proposed broader legislation in 2010. Federal law required aliens who were in the country legally to have registration documents in their possession at all times. But no one made sure they did. SB 1070, which eventually became the Support Our Law Enforcement and Safe Neighborhoods Act, made not having the documents a state crime. The law required police to check the immigration status of people they suspected might be in the country illegally. The police could not stop people for the sole purpose of checking their papers; they could only question people they stopped in the course of their ordinary police activity. People without papers were charged a fine and jailed

Demonstrators march 5 miles (8 km) to Phoenix to protest Arizona's controversial immigration law in May 2010.

until they could show they were in the country legally. Other provisions prohibited illegal aliens from working and authorized their arrest if they were suspected of being guilty of deportable offenses.

As with the California proposition, challenges followed immediately, and a federal judge said that regulation of immigration belonged to the federal government. Opinion in the country was sharply divided, and heated discussion raged for two years. Other states passed similar laws, and opponents staged protest demonstrations and boycotts. In the *Arizona v. United States* (2012) decision, the Supreme Court struck down much of the law, ruling that those parts were preempted by federal legislation. However, the Court upheld the portion that enabled police to check immigration status.

YOUNG ALIENS DREAM

The Supreme Court decision did little to calm emotions or settle the debate. Illegal immigration is a very divisive issue. At one extreme is the idea that anyone in the country illegally has broken the law and needs to be removed. At the other extreme is the belief that there should be few if any restrictions on who can enter the country and enjoy its benefits. Most Americans' views fall somewhere in between.

Many young aliens are caught in the middle. Those who were brought to the United States as children are residents of the United States but citizens of another land they barely know. Their home has nearly always been in America, but for years they had no way of becoming naturalized or even working legally in the United States. What is the best policy for them?

At a 2011 meeting of a Senate subcommittee discussing the proposed DREAM Act, a student silently expresses his hope that senators will decide to pass the legislation.

Congress has attempted to create a pathway for these young illegal immigrants. From 2001 to 2010 legislators proposed three different versions of what they called the DREAM Act, an acronym for Development, Relief, and Education for Alien Minors. The bills outlined ways illegal aliens who came to America as children could become permanent residents. People would be eligible if they lived in the country for at least five years, graduated from a U.S. high school, and either served two years in the U.S. military or attended college for two years. Permanent residency status would qualify them to eventually apply for citizenship.

Those in favor of the DREAM Act cited many social and economic benefits. Opponents called the legislation amnesty and warned that it would encourage more illegal immigration. The opponents won; each time the bill was proposed, it failed. Several individual states have enacted their own versions of the DREAM Act. State laws cannot put aliens on a path to citizenship. However, they can give immigrants who meet their criteria the right to attend state colleges and universities at the same cost as citizens.

REMOVALS ON HOLD

Unhappy with Congress's inability to pass the DREAM Act, President Obama brought out a little-known tool

DREAMS COME TRUE

Carlos Martinez is a "Dreamer." He dreamed of becoming an engineer, making a difference in his community, and being a role model for others. According to an article on HuffingtonPost.com, he worked hard toward those dreams, graduating from high school with a 3.9 grade point average and attending the University of Arizona on scholarships. With both a bachelor's and master's degree, he had job offers at top-notch companies.

But the offers were taken back when the employers learned that Martinez was not authorized to work in the United States. He had come to America illegally when he was nine. The only job he could get was as a manual worker in construction.

When Deferred Action for Childhood Arrivals was announced, Martinez's dream sprang to life again. He immediately started gathering the paperwork he would need to apply for the deferral. As soon as the application process was opened, he submitted his forms. Within a month he received his approval, and then a work permit, and finally a Social Security card. Today he is working at his dream job at IBM.

to give some relief to the children of illegal immigrants. He announced that the U.S. Department of Homeland Security would grant Deferred Action for Childhood Arrivals (DACA). Deferred action is simply a delay; in this case, it is a delay in the enforcement of deportation orders. DACA allows illegal aliens under the age of thirty who meet certain criteria to have their deportations put on hold. They can obtain permission to work in the United States during their deferment. The delay is for a period of two years, but it can be renewed.

Deferred action, like parole, was designed for limited use, on a case-by-case basis, at the discretion of the executive agency, the Department of Homeland Security. The agency exercises "prosecutorial discretion," or the authority to decide which charges to bring and which ones not to pursue. Like parole, deferred action does not grant an immigrant resident status; it merely suspends removal proceedings. Like parole, deferred action is supposed to have an end date, but repeated renewals may render that date meaningless.

As with earlier actions, the announcement of DACA in June 2012 did not solve the immigration problems or end the debate. Congress continues to work toward a policy and practical measures that

On August 15, 2012, the first day DACA applications were accepted, huge crowds formed everywhere applications could be filed. By the end of the year, authorities had received almost 368,000 applications.

will make America more secure and provide some type of legal status for the millions of people living in the country without it.

Much in the immigration discussion has changed over the years. The countries of origin, the places settled, and even the language used to discuss immigration has changed. "Deportation" has become "removal," and many prefer the term "undocumented worker" to "illegal immigrant." Once, immigration policy on citizenship focused on ethnicity. Today, it is largely a question of birthright and legality. Once, residency was about who would be allowed to enter the country. Today, it is about controlling the entrances. Through all the changes, the arguments that arise in the debate are still settled by looking to words penned more than 225 years ago, the words of the Constitution.

GLOSSARY

alien A person who is not a citizen of a country.

amnesty Official pardon.

bill Proposed legislation. The House or the Senate introduces a bill; if the bill becomes a law, it is then called an act.

bipartisan Pertaining to two political parties, typically Democrats and Republicans.

bracero A worker who came from Mexico to work legally in the United States for a limited period of time with a contract through a guest worker program.

commerce The buying and selling of goods.

deportation Removal of an alien from the United States, usually to the last country in which the alien resided.

enumerated power Authority specifically named as belonging to Congress as one of several powers listed in Article 1, Section 8 of the Constitution.

federal Pertaining to the national government rather than to state or local government.

illegal alien An alien who entered the United States illegally, or who entered the United States legally but fell "out of status," violating the length of time or other requirements of a visa. An illegal alien can be deported if apprehended.

immigrant An alien who has been granted the right to live and work in the United States permanently.

landmark decision Judicial ruling that settles a point of law and sets a precedent for how future courts view the particular point.

nativism An anti-immigrant movement in which people who are native-born attempt to exclude those who are foreign-born.

parole power Authority of the executive branch to admit an alien to the United States on a temporary basis for a specific humanitarian purpose.

plenary power Full and complete authority on a particular matter.

preemption The invalidation of a state law because the state law conflicts with a federal law.

ratify To approve formally, especially by signing or voting.

restrictionist Pertaining to the idea that access to the United States should be severely limited.

FOR MORE INFORMATION

Center for Immigration Studies
1629 K Street NW, Suite 600
Washington, DC 20006
(202) 466-8185
Web site: http://www.cis.org
The Center for Immigration Studies is a nonprofit,
    nonpartisan research organization and think tank
    that provides research, opinion, and policy analysis
    of the impacts of immigration.

Constitutional Rights Foundation
601 S. Kingsley Drive
Los Angeles, CA 90005
(213) 487-5590
Web site: http://crf-usa.org
The Constitutional Rights Foundation is a nonprofit,
    nonpartisan organization of teachers and lawyers.
    It provides programs and materials that teach
    young people about the values expressed in the
    Constitution.

The Heritage Foundation
214 Massachusetts Avenue NE
Washington, DC 20002-4999
(202) 546-4400

Web site: http://www.heritage.org

The Heritage Foundation is a conservative research and educational institution that formulates and promotes conservative public policy on a range of issues, including immigration.

Immigration Policy Center
American Immigration Council
1331 G Street NW, Suite 200
Washington, DC 20005-3141
(202) 507-7500
Web site: http://www.immigrationpolicy.org

The Immigration Policy Center is the nonpartisan research arm of the American Immigration Council. It provides information about the role of immigrants and immigration policy in American society.

Migration Policy Institute
1400 16th Street NW, Suite 300
Washington, DC 20036
(202) 266-1940
Web site: http://www.migrationpolicy.org

The Migration Policy Institute is a nonpartisan, non-profit think tank that analyzes the movement of people throughout the world, including into the United States.

National Immigration Forum
50 F Street NW, Suite 300
Washington, DC 20001
(202) 347-0040
Web site: http://www.immigrationforum.org
The National Immigration Forum provides articles,
    reports, and policy advocacy promoting immigra-
    tion and immigrants.

U.S. Citizenship and Immigration Services
20 Massachusetts Avenue NW
Washington, DC 20001
(800) 375-5283
Web site: http://www.uscis.gov
The U.S. Citizenship and Immigration Services is the
    government agency that oversees lawful immigra-
    tion into the United States. It provides information
    and resources about citizenship and naturalization.

WEB SITES

Due to the changing nature of Internet links, Rosen
Publishing has developed an online list of Web sites
related to the subject of this book. This site is updated
regularly. Please use this link to access the list:

http://www.rosenlinks.com/UUSC/Immi

FOR FURTHER READING

Bausum, Ann. *Denied, Detained, Deported: Stories from the Dark Side of American Immigration.* Des Moines, IA: National Geographic, 2009.

Brown, Joanne. *Immigration Narratives in Young Adult Literature: Crossing Borders.* Lanham, MD: Scarecrow Press, 2010.

Budhos, Marina. *Ask Me No Questions.* New York, NY: Atheneum, 2008.

Calavita, Kitty. *Inside the State: The Bracero Program, Immigration, and the I.N.S.* New Orleans, LA: Quid Pro, 2010.

Coan, Peter Morton. *Toward a Better Life: America's New Immigrants in Their Own Words—from Ellis Island to the Present.* Amherst, NY: Prometheus, 2011.

DePietro, Frank. *Latino Americans and Immigration Laws* (Hispanic Americans: Major Minority). Broomall, PA: Mason Crest Publishers, 2013.

Farish, Terry. *The Good Braider.* Tarrytown, NY: Marshall Cavendish, 2012.

Gerber, David A. *American Immigration: A Very Short Introduction.* New York, NY: Oxford University Press, 2011.

Gerdes, Louise I. *Should the U.S. Close Its Borders?* (At Issue). Detroit, MI: Greenhaven Press, 2014.

Golash-Boza, Tanya Maria. *Immigration Nation: Raids, Detentions, and Deportations in Post-9/11 America*. Boulder, CO: Paradigm, 2012.

Gonzalez, Juan. *Harvest of Empire: A History of Latinos in America*. New York, NY: Penguin, 2011.

Haugen, David M., and Susan Musser. *Illegal Immigration* (Opposing Viewpoints). Farmington Hills, MI: Greenhaven, 2011.

Kleyn, Tatyana. *Immigration: The Ultimate Teen Guide*. Lanham, MD: Scarecrow Press, 2011.

Law, Anna O. *The Immigration Battle in American Courts*. New York, NY: Cambridge University Press, 2010.

LeMay, Michael C. *Transforming America: Perspectives on U.S. Immigration*. Santa Barbara, CA: Praeger, 2013.

Levy, Janey. *Illegal Immigration and Amnesty: Open Borders and National Security* (In the News). New York, NY: Rosen Publishing, 2010.

McCormick, Lisa Wade. *Frequently Asked Questions About Growing Up as an Undocumented Immigrant* (FAQ: Teen Life). New York, NY: Rosen Publishing, 2013.

Morrow, Robert. *Immigration: Rich Diversity or Social Burden?* (*USA Today*'s Debate: Voices and Perspectives). Minneapolis, MN: Twenty-First Century Books, 2010.

Perl, Lila. *Immigration: This Land Is Whose Land?* (Controversy!). New York, NY: Marshall Cavendish Benchmark, 2010.

Schrag, Peter. *Not Fit for Our Society: Immigration and Nativism in America.* Berkeley, CA: University of California, 2010.

Schwab, William A. *Right to DREAM: Immigration Reform and America's Future.* Fayetteville, AR: University of Arkansas Press, 2013.

St. John, Warren. *Outcasts United: The Story of a Refugee Soccer Team That Changed a Town.* New York, NY: Delacorte, 2012.

Wong, David H. T. *Escape to Gold Mountain: A Graphic History of the Chinese in North America.* Vancouver, BC, Canada: Arsenal Pulp Press, 2012.

BIBLIOGRAPHY

American Patrol Report. "Calif. Proposition 187 (1994)." Retrieved October 7, 2013 (http://www .americanpatrol.com/REFERENCE/prop187text .html).

American Presidency Project. "Harry S. Truman: Statement by the President upon Signing the Displaced Persons Act, June 25, 1948." Retrieved July 6, 2013 (http://www.presidency.ucsb.edu/ws /?pid=12942).

Cole, Wendy. "Elvira Arellano: An Immigrant Who Found Sanctuary." *Time*, December 25, 2006. Retrieved July 1, 2013 (http://www.time.com /time/specials/packages/article/0,28804,2019341_ 2017328_2017183,00.html).

Constitution Project. "Yick Wo and the Equal Protection Clause." 2013. Retrieved July 1, 2013 (http://www.theconstitutionproject.com/portfolio /yick-wo-and-the-equal-protection-clause).

Daniels, Roger. *Coming to America: A History of Immigration and Ethnicity in American Life*. 2nd ed. New York, NY: Perennial, 2002.

Daniels, Roger. "The Immigration Act of 1965." IIP Digital, U.S. Department of State, April 3, 2008. Retrieved July 2, 2013 (http://iipdigital.usembassy. gov/st/english/publication/2008/04/200804232142 26eaifas0.9637982.html#axzz2YUGr95ag).

Dillingham, William P., and the U.S. Immigration
Commission. "Reports of the Immigration
Commission (1911)." Open Library. Retrieved
July 2, 2013 (http://archive.org/details/reportsof
immigra01unitrich).

Guerrero, Perla. "Heriberto Rivas Lugo." Bracero
History Archive, May 13, 2006. Retrieved July 8,
2013 (http://braceroarchive.org/items/show/273).

Immigration in America. "Displaced Persons Act of
1948." April 10, 2011. Retrieved June 26, 2013
(http://immigrationinamerica.org/464-displaced-
persons-act-of-1948.html?newsid=464).

Justia.com. "Henderson v. Mayor of City of New
York - 92 U.S. 259 (1875)." Retrieved June 24,
2013 (http://supreme.justia.com/cases/federal/us
/92/259/case.html).

Justia.com. "New York v. Miln. 36 U.S. 102 (1837)."
Retrieved July 8, 2013 (http://supreme.justia.com
/cases/federal/us/36/102/case.html).

Justia.com. "Shaughnessy v. Mezei - 345 U.S. 206
(1953)." Retrieved July 10, 2013 (http://supreme
.justia.com/cases/federal/us/345/206/case.html).

Leagle.com. "League of United Latin American
Citizens v. Wilson." 2013. Retrieved July 7, 2013
(http://www.leagle.com/decision/19971428131
F3d1297_11268).

Legal Information Institute, Cornell University Law School. "Plyler v. Doe (No. 80-1538)." Retrieved July 10, 2013 (http://www.law.cornell.edu/supct /html/historics/USSC_CR_0457_0202_ZO.html).

Legal Information Institute, Cornell University Law School. "Scott v. Sandford - 100 U.S. 1." Retrieved July 8, 2013 (http://www.law.cornell.edu/supct /html/historics/USSC_CR_0060_0393_ZS.html).

Lewis, Thomas Tandy. "New York v. Miln." In *Encyclopedia of American Immigration*, edited by Carl L. Bankston III. New Orleans, LA: Tulane University, 2010.

Mazzoli, Romano L., and Alan K. Simpson. "Enacting Immigration Reform, Again." *Washington Post*, September 15, 2006. Retrieved July 12, 2013 (http://www.washingtonpost.com/wp-dyn/content /article/2006/09/14/AR2006091401179.html).

Motomura, Hiroshi, and others. "Letter to the President re: Executive Authority to Grant Administrative Relief for DREAM Act Beneficiaries." May 28, 2012. Retrieved July 8, 2013 (http://www.nilc.org).

Nevarez, Griselda. "Deferred Action Recipient Lands 'Dream Job' a Year after Program's Announcement." *Huffington Post*, June 13, 2013. Retrieved July 17, 2013 (http://www.huffingtonpost.com/2013/06/13 /deferred-action-recipient-job_n_3437530.html).

North American Immigration. "Johnson-Reed Act (1924)." February 21, 2011. Retrieved June 26, 2013 (http://northamericanimmigration.org/173-johnson-reed-act-united-states-1924.html).

North American Immigration. "McCarran-Walter Act (Immigration and Nationality Act) (United States) (1952)." February 22, 2011. Retrieved June 26, 2013 (http://northamericanimmigration.org/195-mccarran-walter-act-immigration-and-nationality-act-united-states-1952.html).

Prengaman, Peter. "Immigration Activist Deported to Mexico." *USA Today*, August 20, 2007. Retrieved July 1, 2013 (http://usatoday30.usatoday.com/news/nation/2007-08-20-2962407204_x.htm).

Preston, Julia. "Number of Illegal Immigrants in U.S. May Be on Rise Again, Estimates Say." *New York Times*, September 23, 2013. Retrieved October 18, 2013 (http://www.nytimes.com/2013/09/24/us/immigrant-population-shows-signs-of-growth-estimates-show.html).

Spaulding, Matthew. "From Pluribus to Unum: Immigration and the Founding Fathers." *Policy Review* 67, Winter 1994, pp. 35–41.

University of North Texas Digital Library. "Congressional Globe: Containing the Debates and Proceedings of the First Session of the

Thirty-Ninth Congress." Retrieved July 1, 2013 (http://digital.library.unt.edu/ark:/67531/ metadc30868).

U.S. Department of Homeland Security. "Border Patrol History." CBP.gov, January 5, 2010. Retrieved July 3, 2013 (http://www.cbp.gov/xp/ cgov/border_security/border_patrol/border_patrol_ ohs/history.xml).

U.S. Department of Homeland Security. "Border Patrol Overview." CBP.gov, January 5, 2011. Retrieved July 3, 2013 (http://www.cbp.gov/xp/ cgov/border_security/border_patrol/border_patrol_ ohs/overview.xml).

U.S. Immigration Legislation Online, University of Washington-Bothell. "U.S. Immigration Legislation: 1917 Immigration Act." Retrieved July 3, 2013 (http://library.uwb.edu/guides/usimmigration/1917 _immigration_act.html).

INDEX

ABOUT THE AUTHOR

Ann Byers is the daughter of a U.S. Customs Service district director and the granddaughter of immigrants from Ireland and France. As a youth worker, she has helped many young immigrants from Southeast Asia and Latin America find jobs; access public services; navigate the educational, health, and legal systems; and adjust to life in America.

PHOTO CREDITS

Cover Craig F. Walker/Denver Post/Getty Images; p. 3 spirit of america/Shutterstock.com; p. 4 Jeff Haynes/AFP/Getty Images; pp. 8, 22, 31, 43, 54, 66, 80 Mikhail Kolesnikov/Shutterstock .com; pp. 10–11Architect of the Capitol; p. 13 Kevork Djansezian /Getty Images; p. 15 Library of Congress Prints and Photographs Division; p. 19 ARC ID 296479. National Archives at San Francisco; p. 23 PhotoQuest/Archive Photos/Getty Images; p. 26 Collection of the Supreme Court of the United States; p. 32 George Eastman House/Archive Photos/Getty Images; p. 37 U.S. National Archives and Records Administration; p. 40 Time & Life Pictures /Getty Images; pp. 44–45 Hulton Archive/Getty Images; p. 49 New York Daily News Archive/Getty Images; p. 51 MPI/Archive Photos/Getty Images; pp. 56–57 Everett Collection/SuperStock; p. 59 J. R. Eyerman/Time & Life Pictures/Getty Images; p. 61 FPG /Archive Photos/Getty Images; pp. 64, 74–75, 84 © AP Images; p. 68 Ernst Haas/Getty Images; p. 71 Roberto Schmidt/AFP/Getty Images; pp. 76–77 Alfredo Sosa/The Christian Science Monitor /Getty Images; pp. 81, 87 Scott Olson/Getty Images; pp. 88–89 Tom Williams/CQ-Roll Call Group/Getty Images; p. 93 Frederic J. Brown/AFP/Getty Images; cover and interior design elements: design36/Shutterstock.com, Eky Studio/Shutterstock.com, Flame of life/Shutterstock.com, Brandon Bourdages/Shutterstock.com; back cover (constitution detail) J. Helgason/Shutterstock.com.

Designer: Michael Moy; Editor: Andrea Sclarow Paskoff;
Photo researcher: Marty Levick